Newly cast handbells awaiting turning and tuning.

GW00362900

HANDBELL

Trevor S. Jennings

Shire Publications Ltd

CONTENTS

Origins and development 3
Handlebells and community life 9
The musical handbell 14
Musical handbells:
   performance and uses 26
Further reading 32
Places to visit 32

Printed in Great Britain by C. I. Thomas & Sons (Haverfordwest) Ltd, Press Buildings, Merlins Bridge, Haverfordwest, Dyfed, SA61 1XF.

British Library Cataloguing in Publication Data: Jennings, Trevor S. (Trevor Stanley). Handbells. 1. Bells. I. Title. 789'.52. ISBN 0-7478-0044-8.

ACKNOWLEDGEMENTS
The author would like to thank the Directors of John Taylor and Company (Bellfounders) Limited for facilities to photograph within the foundry, works and the Bell Foundry Museum; also for permission to use the closed archive. I am indebted to my colleagues in the foundry for advice on moulding procedure. Thanks are also due to my wife Jill Susanna and daughter Amy for helpful suggestions, and to my eldest daughter Emma for some of the illustrations.

Cover: *Handbells of all sizes, old and new, at the Loughborough Bell Foundry of John Taylor and Company.*

This bellringer sounds his handlebells by a dropped-arm method of ringing and appears on a fragment of the Saxon cross discovered at Winwick, Cheshire.

Styles of oriental handlebells. (Left to right) The slashed open bell with engraving dates from about 1850, but the iron temple bell with a decollated edge is over one thousand years old. Circular flanges on the cast brass bell indicate an early Japanese origin, and the small iron bell with a single fingerhold was used as a votive bell in eighteenth-century Burma.

ORIGINS AND DEVELOPMENT

How, when and where man first used small portable bells to create metallic noise, to provide signals and to indicate religious and secular rejoicing and sorrow, is unknown. Crotal bells existed as early as 1500 BC in Egypt and Africa and were basically spherical in shape. They had a hollow body formed by two joined halves and were completely closed except for one or more circular openings or rectangular slits. The crotal could be shaken by means of a small finger grip and the rolling action of a loose metal ball or stone pellet inside the bell made a quiet sound. The earliest bells with an elongated form of handle and a beater or clapper secured to an internal staple came from China, India and Korea and date from 1400 BC. They were usually cast in iron although examples survive in a coarse bronze alloy consisting of copper, tin and zinc.

In 1986 metallurgical analysis of several Indian handlebells made about 1100 BC showed that the proportion of each metal present in the bronze alloy of the bells varied according to the size of the bell and influenced the quality and volume of sound produced. (The term handbell refers to a bell used in musical performance. All other hand-held bells are designated as handlebells). The Chinese were particularly concerned with the tonal quality of their small bells and believed that the different sounds they emitted had miraculous powers. For example, they thought that the significant changes in timbre and musical pitch obtained from various shapes and sizes of bell could influence the forces of nature, assist in curing illness and increase personal happiness and prosperity.

By the fifth century BC Buddhist worshippers used handlebells of many shapes, including those which were domed, oval, pyramidal, round and even square. Whatever their shape, these bells rarely exceeded 150 mm (6 inches) in height and 90 mm (3½ inches) in diameter. They were thick-walled and had a decollated rim which symbolised the lotus flower. Buddhist men were accustomed to present one or more bells to a temple; when the donor died these were sounded during the funeral rites and accompanied him to the grave. Hindu

Hand-held crotal bells spanning three thousand years. The closed spherical bell, based on earlier designs (left), is eighteenth-century AD; the slashed-mouth oval type from China (right) is made of iron and carries an inscription. It dates from 1700 BC.

Left: *A fourteenth-century hammered iron bell with open sides and crown. The metal, which is of uniform thickness, was struck by a long club-shaped clapper.*

Right: *A South American missionary once owned this tall eighteenth-century traveller's bell. Roughly cast in thick yellow brass, it has a primitive cross of native origin for decoration. Attempts to tune the bell can be seen above the rim.*

Left: *A badly cast seventeenth-century bell, possibly of Moorish culture. It has decorated walls of irregular thickness and an open top above the steep sides which supports a primitive and easily dislodged clapper.*

Right: *This early nineteenth-century domed bell has a rectangular tang to receive an optional leather looped handle.*

writings of the fourth century BC record the use of handlebells with a flared outline and an extremely broad rim in the worship of the gods Indra and Parvati. Devotees of the monkey god, Hanuman, rang special bells with handles cast in his image. This gave the ringer the double benefit of contact with the god by touching his likeness and by listening to the sound of the bell.

European bellfounders lacked the inventiveness and metalworking technique of oriental artisans. In Britain between 100 BC and the Roman invasion of AD 43 bells were forged from single plates of iron which varied in thickness. They had an oval or rectangular mouth, were completely plain and had two narrow slits which extended up to within 25 mm (1 inch) of the bell head, where an arched handgrip was formed at right angles to the openings. Travellers and merchants threaded this handgrip on to a leather baldric or waistband, leaving their hands free of the bell. The movement of walking caused the clapper to move across the widest part of the bell mouth and to strike the bell, drawing attention to the arrival of the wearer.

The Romans preferred domed bells with elongated fingerholds and they introduced this pattern wherever their legions conquered and settled. Their sentries were provided with larger and more sonorous bells which they rang to announce the hour of the watch and to warn of an enemy attack. Eventually, to provide greater control over a bell of increased size and weight, for which existing finger and palm grips were insufficient to offer an effective hold, a longer handle was introduced.

A recognisable type of handlebell was thus evolved which, when modified in profile and thickness, became the pattern most widely distributed throughout Europe. Italian house servants were called by bells which had a shorter handle and an additional crossbar. By AD 300 this horizontal bar was thickened and tapered to make a solid projection or tang, which was cast as part of the bell crown, where a separate handle could be secured to the bell by using a ferrule. Clapper supports or crown staples made from loops of thick wire were placed

Left: *A Coptic bell dating from AD 450. It has a flattened, spread rim and a diameter of 57 mm (2¼ inches). The circular stepped handle is surmounted by a projecting finger grip of scrolling ornament. The clapper staple was cast into the bell.*
Right: *An eighth-century quadrangular iron bell with convex riveted sides and a double finger loop. Gold, silver and bronze have been deposited on the exterior at some time, but where the bell wall is thinnest and unprotected there is a corrosion hole.*

within the mould before casting took place. Subsequently the lower part of the handle was carried down through the metal of the bell head to provide a clapper suspension point.

By the time the first Celtic missionary bishops had arrived in Scotland and the north of England about AD 470, all advances in handlebell casting technique had ceased. At his consecration each bishop was presented with a small bell for use in the performance of his episcopal duties. On his death the bell became an object of veneration and was frequently encased in an elaborate shrine and entrusted to the care of an hereditary guardian. Some of these bells and the remains of their jewel-encrusted shrines are preserved in national collections. The most celebrated bell is that attributed to St Patrick which can be seen in the National Museum of Ireland in Dublin. There are similar bells of the same period

but of unestablished ownership in the British Museum and the Victoria and Albert Museum in London.

Such bells weighed about 1 kg (35 ounces) and were forged out of hammered iron using simple blacksmithing methods. A thin iron plate was heated and then beaten into a quadrangular shape, the ends being hammered close or enfolded and secured by welding or by flat studs down one side or both sides, depending upon construction. A bell made of poor-quality iron which has an angular profile produces a weak sound and unmusical tone. Attempts were made to improve the appearance of the bell and its tone by dipping it into melted copper at a temperature approaching 1000 C (1832 F). This superficial coating was not always successful and shedding might occur if the copper covering was thin or applied over a corroded iron surface.

The tall handgrip developed by the

6

Romans was replaced by a narrow double-loop fingerhold later found only on inferior animal bells known as cluckets. Celtic bells were sounded by a method of dropped-arm ringing in which the bells were kept below the ringer's waist and down by his side. Such ringing is regularly depicted in the borders of illuminated medieval manuscripts. A cast bell has more resonance and tonal power than a hammered one and from the seventh century forged iron bells were superseded by those cast in a copper-tin bronze, having domed shoulders, concave sides and a closed crown.

From the beginning of the fifteenth century British bellfounders became more skilful and improved their art to produce a heavier and more robust type of handlebell. In particular the sound-bow, a thickened section of metal located above the rim, was better shaped, allowing the clapper to make a more exact blow. When a taller and thicker handle was supplied the bell could be rung by a full arm movement at shoulder height. By 1500, clappers which had previously been no more than an unshaped mass of irregular section, with a kybe or slight swelling at the lower end to act as a percussive head, now had a shape and weight designed to make a better and louder sound ring out from the bell.

The ubiquitous handlebell had both religious significance and utilitarian purpose in medieval Britain. Bells used at the altar during the celebration of the mass and at benediction and compline remained relatively small and light. Other handlebells which had crown loops or specially prepared tangs could be suspended by strong cord from an angled frame and sounded by one person. This was sometimes done to accompany parts of a church service. The clappers were ignored when the pendant bells were struck on the outside by special beaters. In the streets the handlebell was used to attract the attention of the public. An officially appointed crier announced the time, commented on the weather and proclaimed the latest news as he rang his

Left: *A quadrangular bell showing the method of fastening the folded sides together with studs.*

Right: *An illustration taken from a ninth-century manuscript showing a cleric striking some handlebells which have been placed on a horizontal bar.*

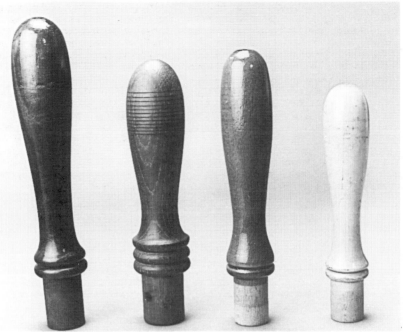

Polished handles for criers' bells in ash, elm and yew wood, 1870-1900. Notice the shapely oak example with fine graining and concentric banding.

bell and perambulated his designated area. Criers' bells were developed to emit a powerful tone and had a clapper made up of a heavy iron ball suspended on a length of closed chain and capable of striking anywhere within the bell.

A thickened crown supported the solid circular boss or wedge-shaped upstand which was prepared to receive a polished wooden handle and its appropriate brass ferrule. Eventually a flat-crowned bell became standard with a simplified handle and clapper staple assembly. This consisted of a threaded rod which passed through the length of the handle, secured above by a decorative nut and inside the bell by an independent crown staple. It became the practice to make the length of the bell handle fractionally longer than the diameter of the bell across its mouth.

Apart from the use of a more refined bell-metal and a flatter crown which makes it easier to locate and secure the handle, the modern handlebell has changed little in form or fittings since the seventeenth century.

Small procession bells with a cast handle would have looked rather like this bell, to judge from the very few descriptions now available to us.

8

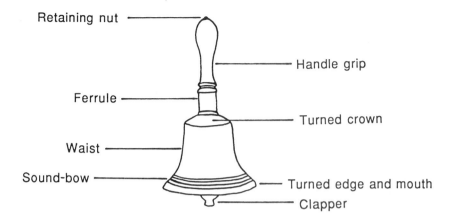

The various parts of a handlebell.

HANDLEBELLS AND COMMUNITY LIFE

Portable bells have played a part in the religious, political and social life of Britain. As many ceremonies and business transactions took place outside where it was either impossible or impracticable to make use of tower-housed bells, the convenience of the handlebell was appreciated and exploited. Towns and villages often had their own customs for the use of handlebells, and local traditions varied considerably. However, certain customs and ringing occasions were common throughout Britain and in Europe.

The medieval beadsman was a minor church official who was paid to walk the parish announcing his presence by ringing a handlebell and, having attracted attention, inviting prayers for the souls of the deceased, the anniversaries of whose deaths fell at that time. References in inventories of church property and churchwarden accounts indicate the use of a substantial bell by the late fifteenth century. It was often more than 4 kg (9 pounds) in weight and maintenance was frequently necessary to the clapper and the handle. Before the Reformation each church was required to provide a bell suitable for ringing before a priest

carrying the sacrament to the housebound. Known as a houseling or call bell, it was usually small and its use was restricted, other handlebells being used for less important functions. For example, the annual Rogationtide perambulation to beat the bounds of the parish and to seek a blessing for the crops was accompanied by the ringing of Rogation bells at the boundary markers. Also known and used as procession bells, they were small and frequently provided in pairs.

By long-standing tradition derived from monastic ritual, lych, forthfare or corse (corpse) bells were sounded by the acolytes who escorted a cortège, as depicted in the Bayeux Tapestry and noted by Chaucer in the *Canterbury Tales*. A small sacring bell, with a cast-on handle (if replica examples favoured by the revivalists of the nineteenth century are historically correct), was rung at the blessing of the sacred elements during the mass, a practice first recorded in the twelfth century. Sometimes sacring bells were reserved for use at a particular altar specified by a benefactor. Otherwise referred to as sanctus or saunce bells,

9

some were cast in pierced metal after a Byzantine style and decorated with an angel, lion, ox and eagle, symbols of the four evangelists. The most prestigious and best endowed churches had separate handlebells of various sizes and different notes for use in chantry chapels, at the time of harvest or excommunication. All these bells were wantonly destroyed or secularised at the Reformation as they were held to be superstitious ornaments. Iconoclastic vandalism, followed by changes in public worship, effectively ended the use of the handlebell in religious observance in the established church until the mid nineteenth century.

To medieval ears the tinkling sound of handlebells signalled the approach of a traveller or of someone physically afflicted, seeking alms and sympathy; during plague visitations, larger bells sounded the arrival of the mortality cart. Easily accessible warning or fire bells alerted inhabitants to disasters of various kinds and during the Civil Wars of 1642-

Above: Acolytes ring their handbells dropped-arm fashion beside the funeral bier of King Edward the Confessor, as portrayed in the Bayeux Tapestry.

Below left: A cast bronze sacring bell with detailed workmanship. The fine quatrefoil handle is in the Gothic Revival style of the 1840s.

Below right: A Byzantine-style sacring bell of the early nineteenth century, with highly decorative pressed bodywork and a sigmoid handle set on the stepped head. When the bell was converted into an inkstand it was cut through above the inscription band to form a hinged lid.

48 were used to warn of nearby military action. These bells were rung with the arm raised so that the clapper struck with full force in a forward blow. Deliberate misuse of the warning bell was a punishable offence.

The unfortunate men lying in the condemned cell of Newgate Prison in London were aroused at midnight on the eve of their execution by St Sepulchre's bellman warning of doom, calling for repentance and ringing his long-handled bell to reinforce his message.

Eighteenth-century criers' bells had good carrying power and were provided with substantial wooden handles, some over 30 cm (12 inches) in length, specially turned so that they could be grasped with both hands. A century later similar bells were used on railway station platforms to announce the arrival and departure of trains. During the First World War the government placed contracts with bell-founders for oval-mouthed bells for use by the Army. In place of a solid wooden handle there was a flexible strap made of webbed material for threading on to a

This execution bell was rung outside the condemned cell at Newgate Prison in London by the bellman of St Sepulchre. He then recited verses calling upon the condemned prisoners to repent of their crimes. The custom originated in a bequest of 1605.

Four handlebells used for different purposes. The tall bell with double handgrip weighs 5.4 kg (12 pounds). It belonged to the railway station at Holbeach, Lincolnshire, and dates from 1862. To the right of it is a thinner auctioneer's bell with a frail mouth split from excessive use. The two bells on the left were for street trading and school use.

11

Left: *Dating from 1940, this air raid precaution warden's bell was made at the Fiddian bell foundry of James Barwell in Birmingham. It has a turned edge and crown, with an oak handle and inscribed ferrule, and weighs 3.4 kg (7½ pounds).*
Right: *A gas-attack warning bell used in the trenches during the First World War, 1914-18. A truncated and flattened cone shape, it has a thick mouth and its original webbed handle strap.*

belt and these bells were worn by officers moving through the trenches to warn of an imminent gas attack. In the Second World War bells were issued to designated air-raid wardens throughout Britain who rang them to alert the residents of their patrol area of a possible bombing attack.

Some itinerant street traders, market stallholders and auctioneers still use handlebells. They can be frequently heard at the Saturday street market in Loughborough, Leicestershire, and at cattle auctions in Leicestershire and Nottinghamshire. These noisy bells with heavy wrought iron ball clappers are considered to be indispensable tools of the trade and are regarded as heirlooms, frequently being handed down through successive generations. Some publicans in the East Midlands ring handlebells to signal closing time and in many Leicestershire schools the teachers use a crier's bell to bring in the children at the start of lessons.

Bells with looped handles made of spring steel may be seen in country districts suspended from a framework erected across a minor road or farm track leading to a railway level crossing where there are overhead power cables. Vehicles with tall loads which would foul these cables cannot pass beneath the bells without causing them to sound and so warn the driver that it is dangerous to proceed further.

By removing the wooden handles and replacing them with a strip of spring steel,

Above left: *A schoolroom bell with characteristic short handle and hammered copper ferrule. This type of small bell was used in early nineteenth-century monitor-system schooling.*

Above right: *Busy servants in a gentleman's house would have hurried to obey the sound of this nineteenth-century call bell. Its spring-steel handle and gilded centre boss are secured to a piece of the original indicator board.*

Below: *Three table and call bells. The eighteenth-century broad-mouthed bell of iron (left) has a superior and independent handle of fleur-de-lis and contrasts with the taller inferior bell with its cheap moulded grip (right). In the centre is a fine Victorian crinoline bell showing meticulous attention to fashion detail.*

13

many bells were modified for other purposes. The Victorians summoned their servants by activating one or more bells connected by a pulley system throughout the house to an indicator board, and shopkeepers installed tell-tales above their doors to announce the arrival of a customer. Personal or table bells were the smallest of all handlebells and were usually cast separately from the handle, which was screwed or brazed to the crown. Made with decorative handholds of ivory, porcelain or wood, they were produced in many different shapes by brassfounders and artisans. Some were formed in the shape of a crinolined lady, her legs becoming the clapper, and were highly polished for giving as marriage presents. Small handlebells remain popular as souvenirs of some special occasion or visit.

Town criers can be heard today in many towns, including Leicester, Melton Mowbray (Leicestershire) and Manchester. They are more for the benefit of tourists than local people for the handlebell and its message have largely ceased to have significance in modern life.

THE MUSICAL HANDBELL

Most types of larger handlebell cast for specific purposes were noisy, robust and entirely unsuitable for musical performance. However, they were the precursors of the tuned handbell which was developed in Britain throughout the eighteenth century. Completely redesigned and tonally enhanced, musical handbells were handcrafted instruments, individually made to customers' requirements. Available in diatonic and chromatic sets, forming a complete percussion instrument, the range was capable of extension by adding several smaller or larger bells to the existing sequence. Diatonic sets could be augmented by the addition of suitable semitone bells.

After 1700 radical changes in production became possible when British foundrymen introduced new casting techniques. The moulds were no longer struck up in loam using a shaped crook or template or by lost-wax methods but were produced from full-sized reusable patterns placed directly into moulding boxes. The immediate benefits were speed of manufacture, economy of production and a superior bell. In the late nineteenth century the moulder who worked in the handbell-casting department of John Taylor's bell foundry at Loughborough was scheduled to prepare 32 moulding boxes a day, each containing a minimum of twelve patterns. Such was the volume of trade at that time.

Over-coppered alloys were gradually phased out in favour of a more balanced but brittle bronze composition of 77 per cent copper and the balance of pure tin. This was ideal for handbells with an improved profile and thinner cross-section. Consequently many early handbells of uncertain pitch with thick rounded shoulders and flared mouths were consigned to the melting pot as owners updated their sets.

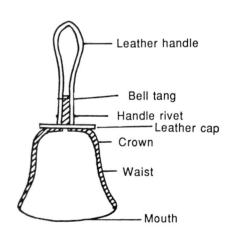

Leather handle

Bell tang

Handle rivet
Leather cap

Crown

Waist

Mouth

The various parts of a musical handbell.

14

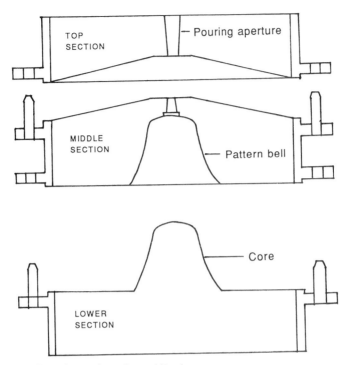

TOP SECTION — Pouring aperture

MIDDLE SECTION — Pattern bell

Core

LOWER SECTION

The cross-section through a triple-stack moulding box.

Modern handbells are cast in moulding boxes made up of several sections. When a triple stack is used each part is separated before the metal bell patterns are placed mouth downwards on a board located beneath the middle section. Specially prepared sand is sieved over them and the box is tightly rammed, but leaving the pattern tops visible. Any surplus sand is removed before trowelling the remainder to a clean finish and covering it with parting powder or fine sand. This ensures a clean separation from the upper section of the box, which is next prepared as a pouring cavity to connect with the ingate or metal entrance. The two completed sections are firmly secured together and inverted to reveal the bell patterns, mouth upwards. A pair of bellows is used to clean out any undesirable moulding material from the inside of each pattern bell. The lower section of the box is then rammed up to take the inside shape of the patterns and so form the cores.

With the box the correct way up, the topmost section is carefully removed and the pattern heads are lightly tapped before the middle portion is raised and the patterns are extracted. Each core is now exposed and sprayed with a thin film of oil to prevent leaching of metal into the moulding sand when casting takes place. Lubricant is also run over the head of the separate cores to act as a shield against initial damage when the metal is introduced into the mould. Moulding is now complete and the box is reassembled and each section wedged into place. Pricking the sand for ventilation will reduce the possibility of a porous casting, and weights placed on the box will counteract any premature rising due to pressure caused when the hot metal enters through the prepared and bushed apertures.

Sufficient bell-metal to complete the casting is heated in a resistant crucible to

Above: *Three pattern bells stand on the moulding board within the middle section of the box, and fine sand is sieved over them at the start of the moulding process.*

Below: *Sand now covers the pattern bells and the moulding-box section is full. The sand will be consolidated by ramming up.*

a temperature exceeding 1100 C (2012 F) by means of a pot furnace. Crucible management and subsequent pouring of the metal are by hand, after which the castings are left to cool naturally. On the following day the box is dismantled and the bells are retrieved after separation from the header bar, formed when the metal was poured in. Castings need fettling down with a stiff wire brush to remove hard-baked moulding material adhering to their rough surface.

Turning, to a highly polished finish, followed by tuning on a horizontal lathe, removes excess metal from all parts of the bell. Allowance is made for this by casting the handbell thicker in body, and sharper in note, than the required finished product. No polishing lacquer is used as this detracts from musical quality. Older handbells were tuned to the pitch of the bellfounder's choice and could vary considerably. Handbells produce several notes when struck, but only two are significant and these must be brought into correct musical relationship. Pitch is

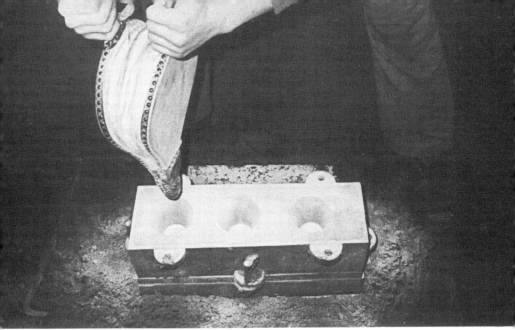

Hand bellows with a fine-bore nozzle are used to remove any parting powder from the inside of each pattern before the cores can be moulded.

It is a delicate operation to withdraw the pattern bells from the newly formed cores without damaging them.

After the cores have been sprayed with a thin film of oil and a thicker lubricant has been put on to the heads the mould is closed down.

The mould is complete and must now be pricked to increase ventilation before casting takes place.

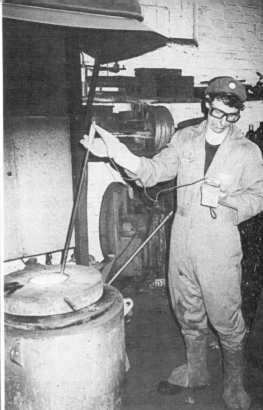

Left: *Completed moulding boxes containing three bells have been prepared for individual casting and await the arrival of the molten metal. The pouring apertures are covered to prevent the intrusion of unwanted material and to exclude dampness.*

Right: *The pyrometer has been placed into the molten metal in the crucible within the pot furnace. This will measure the temperature, which should reach 1100 C (2012 F) before any casting can take place.*

determined by the fundamental or strike note, by which the bell is known, and the twelfth, which is a loud and identifiable harmonic or tone, one octave and seven semitones higher. Tuning small bells in high frequencies calls for accuracy and skill, without over-reduction of the thickness of the bell wall. A sensitive ear and the expert use of tuning forks and electronic equipment permit accuracy to within one-hundredth of one semitone. Handbells increase in size according to the depth of their strike note, and a short set forms a complex musical instrument in which each bell receives individual tuning yet must be tonally related to all the other bells.

In keeping with tradition, a fine leather handgrip is provided, its width and length specific to each bell, and this is attached by a copper rivet to the projecting tang on the bell crown. Tanned leather handles are comfortable to hold and permit controlled manipulation of the bell. They can be made firmer by layering the strap leather or by inserting a harder but flexible material such as copper strip. A strong circular leather cap or handguard, tooled in simple patterns and pierced to accommodate the tang, protects the crown and prevents the accidental damping of sound by contact with the hand. Before the mid nineteenth century caps were made out of soft thin leather and fell over the shoulders of the handbell.

The crucible containing the molten metal is removed from the pot furnace with special tongs and prepared for hand casting.

Casting small bells at the Whitechapel Bell Foundry in the early nineteenth century. Notice the hand crucible method of pouring the molten metal. This famous bell foundry has produced handbells of the highest quality since the eighteenth century.

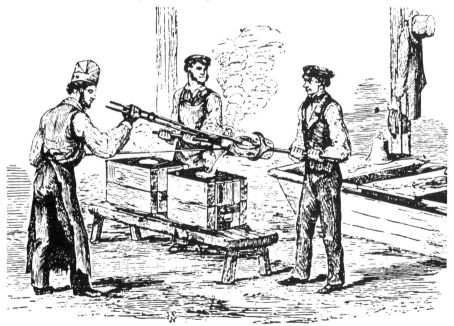

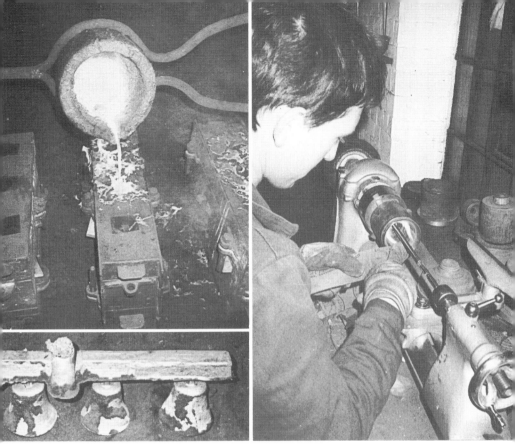

Top left: *A thin fiery stream of molten bell-metal is carefully poured by hand from the crucible into the moulds, filling the air with cupric and stannic gases.*

Above left: *Newly cast handbells still attached to the runner bar. The moulding sand has yet to be removed by fettling from their rough surface, and the cores have to be extracted.*

Right: *Fine tuning is carried out by removing metal from the interior of the handbell. This process requires a combination of engineering skills and musical intuition.*

Each handbell has a detachable and renewable clapper assembly threaded into the bell crown, consisting of a forked staple and two brass springs secured by rivets. Early brass retaining springs were long stiff blades with spade-like terminations, very different from the modern laser-cut forms. The felted ends on the inside of each spring control sound production and effectively regulate movement of the clapper within one plane across the mouth of the bell and prevent it from hitting any other part of the bell interior, as happens with criers' bells.

Once the clapper has delivered its blow the springs make it rebound off the sound bow and allow the bell to vibrate freely and also ensure that the clapper is immediately available for reuse during the performance of a piece of music.

In the early decades of the twentieth century bellfounders gave much thought to the improvement of clapper assemblies. John William Taylor's contribution was the tapping of a small screw into the side of the tang to prevent the whole action from turning round and becoming loose.

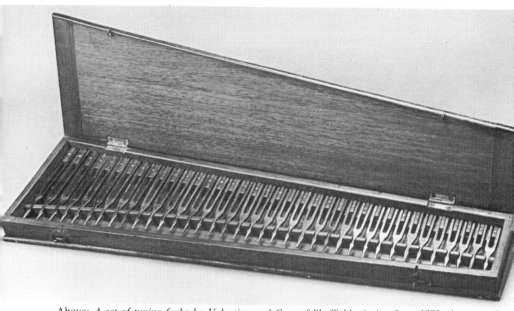

Above: *A set of tuning forks by Valentine and Carr of Sheffield. Dating from 1880, they extend over three chromatic octaves. This set has its own custom-made carrying case and was used exclusively for the tuning of handbells.*

Below left: *The electronic tuning being carried out on a handbell is nearing completion. The bell's correct pitch will be within one cent, or one-hundredth of a semitone.*

Below right: *Each handbell in this set has been tuned and is suspended to prevent damage occurring to the mouth whilst waiting for the clapper assembly and handle to be fitted.*

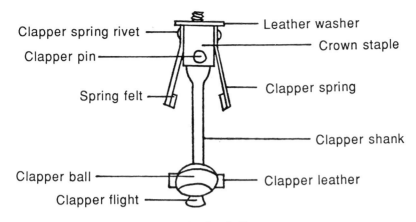

Clapper spring rivet

Clapper pin

Spring felt

Clapper ball

Clapper flight

Leather washer

Crown staple

Clapper spring

Clapper shank

Clapper leather

A modern bell-clapper assembly used in English handbells.

Clappers which are too long, over-strong or badly positioned induce spring fatigue at the rivet point. Early clappers had shanks of iron or brass, with a percussive ball of hardwood or metal, and lacked a cushioned striking arrangement. From the late eighteenth century clapper balls have been bored to accept inserts of leather, and more recently nylon, depending on bell size. Those of larger bells are felted, or covered in chamois leather, to ensure optimum tonal balance. Small bells require a hard striking surface for the same reason. Resin

Four clapper assemblies dating from 1750 to 1880, illustrating the evolution of the restraining spring from an adze-shaped or thick pointed termination to a broader and more resilient form. Clapper balls range from a hardwood variety to those of iron, felted or flightless. Notice the unusual leather hinge on the clapper with the iron spherical ball (second from the left).

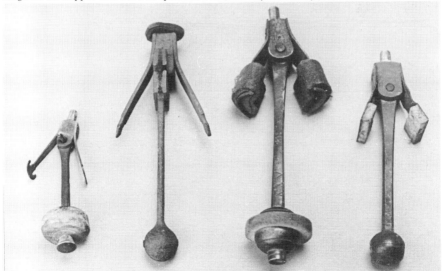

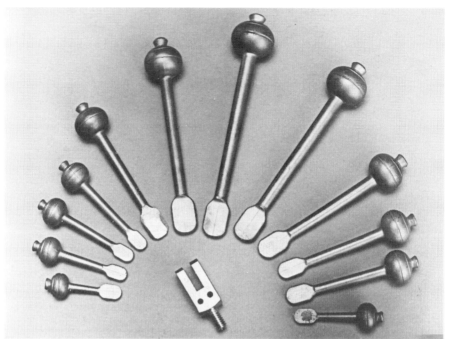

Modern clapper blanks of a standard shape, graduated in size for use in a short set of handbells; the crown staple shown is that for the largest clapper.

These bells illustrate improvements in handbell shape. The seventeenth-century loam-cast Italian bell (left), with the Messina crest, has a thick soundbow compared to the sand-cast Aldbourne Foundry handbell of over a century later. The bells are identical in diameter and height, but the Italian bell is 0.9 kg (2 pounds) heavier.

Left: *An early mid-Victorian portrait of Abraham Quail, who fitted up the handbell sets for John Taylor as well as working as a bellhanger.*

Right: *A fine handbell, 151mm (6 inches) in diameter, with the well proportioned profile characteristic of Henry Symondson's work, which was admired by many mid nineteenth-century ringers.*

compositions are used in the manufacture of American handbell fittings, which differ considerably from British types, especially in their clapper movements, which are made up of many small parts and have alternative securing devices.

Many bellfounders began making handbells after 1700 and imitated the work of the Cor family of Aldbourne in Wiltshire, who used solid patterns for their bell moulds. The work of the Cors can be identified by the initials WC cast in raised lettering on the inside of the bells; this made tuning impossible at that point, although filing was carried out elsewhere. Robert Wells and his sons succeeded to this business, improved the Cors' patterns and continued the unorthodox practice of using internal initials. The Aldbourne clientele widened consider-

ably and numerous small sets of bells were cast until 1825, when the patterns and plant were purchased by Thomas Mears II of London. From the early nineteenth century provincial bell-founders, such as John Rudhall of Gloucester and Taylors at Oxford and Loughborough, supplied an ever increasing market, but the London companies of John Warner and Thomas Mears captured the greatest proportion of the trade.

Part-time artisans, such as Henry Symondson in the nineteenth century, worked from small premises supplying musical handbells singly or in sets. A former tuner of church bells and an accomplished London theatre violinist, Symondson had his bells cast to particular patterns, receiving the castings back for personal tuning and fitting up at his workshop behind his house in Tottenham Court Road, London. His son Philip, the Londoners George Stockham and George Welsh and the Yorkshireman John Mallaby all made use of his excellent patterns, for Symondson-profile bells were acknowledged as superior. From the mid nineteenth century enthusiastic handbell groups in the north of England patronised the Bradford bellfounder James Shaw, who on several occasions provided long sets of over two hundred bells. Midland ringers were served by the Birmingham bell foundries of James Barwell, William Blews and Charles Carr.

Today handbells for Britain and other countries are supplied by fewer than twenty bellfounders and sundry small producers and assemblers who use the finest materials, precision engineering skills and advanced electronic tuning methods. However, it is the purity of sound that decides the quality of any handbell, large or small, not its method of production, and the skill of the tuner is very important.

MUSICAL HANDBELLS: PERFORMANCE AND USES

The first musical handbells were used by people who wished to practise change ringing in more congenial surroundings than the ringing room in an austere church tower. As change ringing increased in popularity the possession of a set of handbells, equivalent to the tower bells in number and musical sequence though not exact note, was considered an asset and they were often purchased with belfry funds. Eighteenth-century publicans also bought sets of bells, which were kept on the premises and used by regular groups of players who formed societies unconnected with any church. Such ringing, a form of chamber music, became a social activity. By judicious augmentation the band could ring a wider variety of methods than simple rounds and perform melodies which fell within the range of the bells. With three octaves or more, harmonised tune ringing was accomplished. It was through earnest ringing bands, not encouragement from church authorities, that handbells became popular, affordable and accepted as legitimate musical instruments.

Many sets of handbells were purchased by private owners who formed ringing societies and gave public performances. In the eighteenth century ringing competitions with prizes of gloves, hats and miscellaneous goods, formerly restricted to performances on church-tower bells, were extended to include handbells. Strictly secular competitions were orga-

nised along the lines of major established music festivals, but the greatest impetus came from tune-ringing bands concentrated in the northern counties of Britain. The most prestigious annual event was the Handbell Ringing Contest, which took place at Belle Vue Gardens, Manchester, between 1855 and 1926. It was a gathering of acclaimed handbell-ringing talent, second only in importance to the national brass-band competition and attracting large audiences.

With maximum attention focused on musicianship and not change-ringing expertise, well qualified musicians were engaged to adjudicate in preference to eminent personalities of the ringing Exercise. Rules were strict, and competitors obtaining three consecutive first places were refused admission the following year.

The bell orchestra, sometimes erroneously termed a carillon, was a Victorian phenomenon firmly established by the 1880s, by groups which possessed up to 250 bells. Many sets of bells were remodelled tonally and numerically, and bellfounders' records indicate that bells originally intended for sheep, the hame boxes on horse collars or to summon servants were sent to foundries for tuning and modification. By the addition of caps, handles and clapper assemblies such bells were converted into instruments for musical performance. Some duplication of bells was necessary for

26

A diatonic set of eight handbells hang on a bar for tapping purposes. This arrangement was useful in church-tower ringing rooms to demonstrate new methods of change ringing before making an attempt on the tower bells.

A hame box from a horse collar containing four tuned bells cast by Robert Wells in the late eighteenth century. The handbell, from the same foundry, illustrates how such horse bells could be converted to musical use.

advanced part playing and specially transcribed bell music, the first recorded instance being at Belle Vue in 1886. Several groups attained a remarkably high standard of tune ringing, offering unique entertainment that was sufficiently pleasing for them to be asked to appear before invited guests at royal functions. By 1876 the Royal Portland Street Handbell Ringers had given six command performances, their tune ringing being far removed from the first melodies published for handbells in the mid nineteenth century by Daniel Schofield.

Smaller and high-pitched musical handbells are treated as transposing instruments, producing sounds one

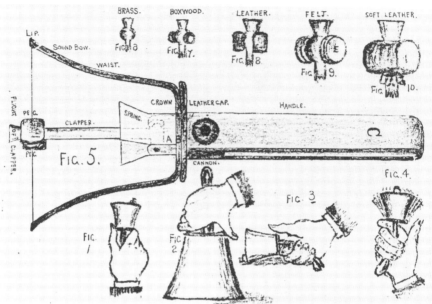

No. 6. — Whistling Farmer Boy.

Above: This illustration comes from William Gordon's nineteenth-century treatise on musical handbell ringing. Note the various types of clapper plug and the handgrip positions.

Left: Two nineteenth-century methods of composing for handbell ringers. The extract from 'Whistling Farmer Boy' makes use only of numerals, each figure representing one bell within the octave. Player five rang his bell only when that figure appeared on the sheet and took his musical time from the system of dots, commas and colons. The second extract is part of a musical score arranged for a large bell orchestra. The figures and letters refer to the position of bells on the table and not to particular notes or players.

octave higher than the written score, which otherwise would contain far too many ledger-lines. The tonal and technical limitations of handbells require a carefully selected repertoire, transcribed and adapted for the particular use of each individual group of ringers.

Sound alone is not sufficient, for timing, rhythmic precision, expression and uniformity in the weight of striking between the ringers are factors of prime importance. All percussion instruments produce sound which reverberates to natural decay unless terminated abruptly,

Above: *The Loughborough Campanological Band of 1887 giving a concert in the grounds of Bellfoundry House to commemorate the Golden Jubilee of Queen Victoria. Notice the off-the-table style of ringing.*

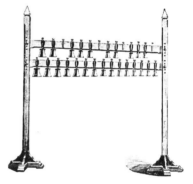

Right: *A typical handbell tapping stand used by solo performers. The bells were interchangeable from one rail to the other to facilitate the performance of tunes in different keys.*

and handbell ringers can easily blur harmonic backgrounds with insensitive attention to detail. Compositions can be presented in musical staff notation, tonic solfa, or by using coloured and marked notes which enable a ringer to differentiate an individual part. Systems of numeration and alphabet shorthand also exist, which replace standard notation for the musically untutored. All these methods are used today.

There are two distinct styles of ringing handbells; in-hand and off-the-table. In-hand methods involve holding either one or two bells in each hand. Two bells in one hand are held at right angles to each other so that one is sounded by a downward movement and the other by a sideways action. Groups wishing to limit the number of ringers but perform with many handbells develop an off-the-table method of performance. The bells are placed on a well padded table in front of the ringers, who are each responsible for several bells. Lifted from the table, the bell is sounded and then returned, none being kept in the hand. Lapping, where the bells are held in the lap of the performer, and rolling, in which the bells are passed or rolled along the table to another ringer, were methods now regarded as inferior.

The tune player and the peal tapper were true soloists. Their performances were usually executed on a two-octave set of handbells suspended from a specially

29

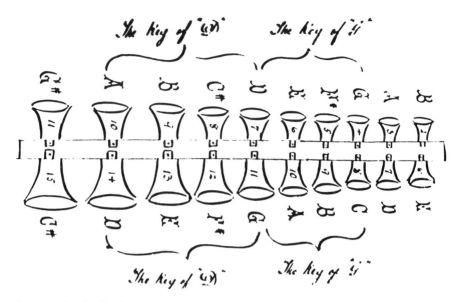

A manuscript sketch of 1866 setting out the disposition of twenty handbells to form a dulcimer capable of playing in the keys of G and D major, with a few additional notes.

The Lancashire Ringers performed at the Adelphi Theatre, London, in 1843. Their conductor, Henry Johnson, used his violin bow as a baton.

constructed stand or frame. The bells were sounded by two felt-covered disc hammers on thin handles. The most famous peal tapper was Elijah Roberts, born in 1807, who was skilled in the art by the age of twelve. He was brass-founder, a stagecoach guard and later a publican and his greatest feat was 19,440 changes on twelve bells in just under fourteen hours of continuous ringing in

1864. The handbell dulcimer was a popular Victorian drawing-room and music-hall instrument. Two horizontal rows of bells, grouped in key sequence, were set within a large resonating box with their mouths facing outwards, each strap and tang being supported on a central wooden strut. The bells were struck by tapping sticks made of hickory wood or even ebony or teak.

From the buffoonery of circus performers to the sophistication of the serious ringing band and the entertainment provided by well known and popular musical families, handbells were continually presented to the public on equal terms with traditional orchestral instruments. The Walford family of Bletchingley, Surrey, owned over two hundred Taylor bells and incorporated them into classical scores for their concerts.

In churches lacking organ or instrumental music, clergymen occasionally engaged a handbell group to accompany the services. The group's conductor, who usually did not perform, kept time with a violin bow in nineteenth-century orchestral fashion. Musical and well presented handbell groups were often called upon to perform at private house parties given by affluent public celebrities. In contrast, they might be requested to ring at a graveside as a gesture of respect.

Simple music is adequately performed on a short set of handbells and as early as 1920 therapists working in a number of medically related disciplines amongst the blind, disabled and mentally ill encouraged their patients to participate in ringing. Teachers, too, encouraged their pupils of all ages and abilities to take part in handbell ringing for musical pleasure and learning. Music prizes sometimes took the form of a set of handbells, suitably inscribed and presented in a custom-made box. Many such sets were supplied by bellfounders from 1920 to 1936.

National and socio-economic pressures led to a great decline in handbell performance but a revival of interest began in 1967 with the establishment of the Handbell Ringers of Great Britain, who have fostered and encouraged the formation of many groups. The unique combination of historical, musical and social attributes expressed through handbell performance had appealed to American

Sets of handbells are costly instruments to produce and are easily damaged. Prudent owners protect their bells from accidental damage by keeping them in a custom-made box. This substantial wooden container holds a chromatic octave of thirteen bells. Some modern cases have a cushioned lining.

church groups from the time when the showman Phineas T. Barnum engaged English ringers to perform on his entertainment tours. Today large handbell choirs flourish and cultivate high standards of ringing. In 1988 the third International Handbell Symposium was held in Exeter, Devon, bringing together groups of performers from many countries, including Australia, Canada, Japan and Korea — the Eastern influence of earlier centuries coming full circle.

The handbell is a universal instrument, capable of high-class playing in a variety of styles by ringers of every age and specialism. Its study requires no long academic tuition but a musical dedication and a willingness to be directed by group instruction. Viewed historically, the handbell is among the world's longest surviving musical instruments.

FURTHER READING

Camp, J. *Discovering Bells and Bellringing*. Shire Publications, third edition 1988.
Fletcher, C. W. *Handbell Ringing*. J. Curwen and Sons, London, 1888.
Jennings, T. S. *Bellfounding*. Shire Publications, 1988.
Jennings, T. S. *The Taylor Bell Foundries 1784-1987*. The Bell Foundry Museum, 1987.
Morris, E. *Tintinnabula*. Robert Hale, 1959.
Price, P. *Bells and Man*. Oxford University Press, 1983.
Spear, N. *A Treasury of Archaeological Bells*. Hastings House, New York, 1978.
Tufts, N. P. *The Art of Handbell Ringing*. Herbert Jenkins, 1962.
Walters, H. B. *Church Bells of England*. Oxford University Press, 1912; reprinted E. P. Publishing, 1977.
Walters, H. B. *The Church Bells of Wiltshire*. Kingsmead Reprints, Bath, 1969.

The reader is also referred to specific articles in *Reverberations,* the official journal of the Handbell Ringers of Great Britain. Further information can be obtained from the Secretary, Roger A. Lazenby, 2 Holt Park Approach, Leeds, West Yorkshire, LS16 7PW.

PLACES TO VISIT

Many museums, national and local, contain examples of small handlebells and related items. Those listed below have specific collections. Intending visitors are advised to find out the times of opening before making a special journey.

The Bell Foundry Museum, Freehold Street, Loughborough, Leicestershire LE11 1AR. Telephone: 0509 233414. A unique museum relating to all aspects of bellfounding. Tours of the world's largest working bell foundry are available for parties by appointment.

Dorset County Museum, High West Street, Dorchester, Dorset DT1 1XA. Telephone: 0305 62735. Collection of local animal and horse-harness bells.

Salisbury and South Wiltshire Museum, The King's House, 65 The Close, Salisbury, Wiltshire SP1 2EN. Telephone: 0722 332151. Details of Aldbourne Foundry and many artefacts.